GRAND CANYON

National Park

BY CHRISTINA LEAF

BLASTOFF!
DISCOVERY

BELLWETHER MEDIA • MINNEAPOLIS, MN

Blastoff! Discovery launches a new mission: reading to learn. Filled with facts and features, each book offers you an exciting new world to explore!

BLASTOFF! UNIVERSE

BLASTOFF! Beginners
GRADE K

BLASTOFF! READERS
GRADES 1-3

BLASTOFF! DISCOVERY
GRADE 4

This edition first published in 2023 by Bellwether Media, Inc.

No part of this publication may be reproduced in whole or in part without written permission of the publisher.
For information regarding permission, write to Bellwether Media, Inc.,
Attention: Permissions Department,
6012 Blue Circle Drive, Minnetonka, MN 55343.

Library of Congress Cataloging-in-Publication Data

Names: Leaf, Christina, author.
Title: Grand Canyon National Park / by Christina Leaf.
Other titles: Blastoff! discovery. U.S. National Parks.
Description: Minneapolis, MN : Bellwether Media, Inc., 2023. |
    Series: Blastoff! Discovery: U.S. National Parks | Includes bibliographical
    references and index. | Audience: Ages 7-13 | Audience: Grades 4-6 |
    Summary: "Engaging images accompany information about Grand Canyon
    National Park. The combination of high-interest subject matter and narrative
    text is intended for students in grades 3 through 8"–Provided by publisher.
Identifiers: LCCN 2022016477 (print) | LCCN 2022016478 (ebook) |
    ISBN 9781644877531 (library binding) | ISBN 9781648347993 (ebook)
Subjects: LCSH: Grand Canyon National Park (Ariz.)-Juvenile literature.
Classification: LCC F785.7 .L43 2023 (print) | LCC F785.7 (ebook) |
    DDC 979.1/32–dc23
LC record available at https://lccn.loc.gov/2022016477
LC ebook record available at https://lccn.loc.gov/2022016478

Editor: Betsy Rathburn
Series Design: Jeffrey Kollock   Book Designer: Laura Sowers

Printed in the United States of America, North Mankato, MN.

TABLE OF CONTENTS

GRAND CANYON
NATIONAL PARK

NATIONAL
PARK
SERVICE

THE NORTH RIM

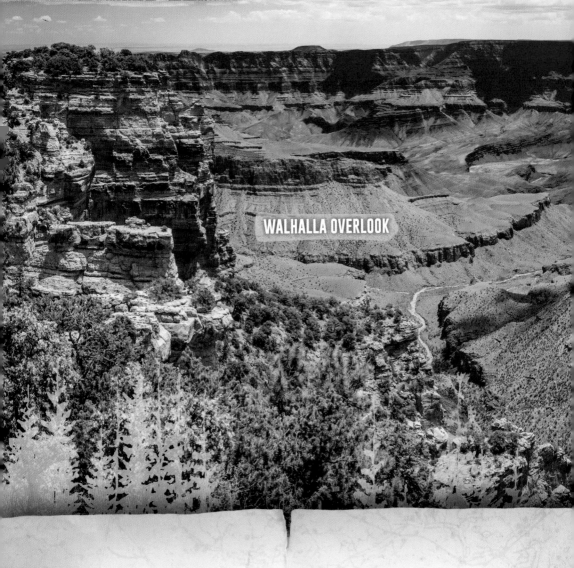

WALHALLA OVERLOOK

A family is ready to explore the North Rim of the Grand Canyon! They start at the Walhalla Overlook. The canyon stretches out before them. Stripes of red and purple paint the steep walls and **mesas**. Far below, small streams wind through **ravines**. It is hard to believe how huge the canyon is!

WALHALLA GLADES

Eventually, they cross the road to visit Walhalla Glades. **Ancestral** Puebloans once lived at this site each summer to farm. The family imagines the buildings that rose from the stones that remain. Grand Canyon National Park is full of beauty and history!

GRAND CANYON NATIONAL PARK

Grand Canyon National Park preserves one of the natural wonders of the world. Located in north-central Arizona, the park covers 1,878 square miles (4,864 square kilometers). The Navajo Nation and the Hualapai and Havasupai **Reservations** border the park. The powerful Colorado River flows through the canyon.

Grand Canyon's awe-inspiring views make it one of the country's most popular national parks. Most visitors enjoy the views from the South Rim of the Grand Canyon. Others head to the North Rim, or trek down to the canyon floor.

NORTH RIM

SOUTH RIM

N
W—E
S

COLORADO
RIVER

ARIZONA

= GRAND CANYON
NATIONAL PARK

HOW BIG?

The Grand Canyon stretches 277 miles (446 kilometers) long. It is up to 18 miles (29 kilometers) wide and can reach more than 1 mile (1.6 kilometers) deep!

SOUTH RIM

THE LAND

A TRIP THROUGH TIME

Visitors can view the many different layers of rock on the canyon walls. The youngest rock layer is 270 million years old!

The Grand Canyon began forming almost 2 billion years ago. **Igneous** and **metamorphic** rock covered the ground. Over time, layers of **sedimentary** rock formed on top. Eventually, the area was pushed upward, forming the Colorado **Plateau**. Around 5 or 6 million years ago, the mighty Colorado River began to carve the Grand Canyon.

The river cut through the rock quickly. Its rushing waters carried rocks that wore down the sedimentary layers underneath. Small streams and **runoff** from the rim caused **erosion**, widening the canyon. Today, erosion from water and wind continue to shape the canyon.

COLORADO RIVER

RIVER EROSION

1. Water movement picks up and carries rocks and sand.

2. Moving rocks and sand wear away more pieces of the riverbed.

RIVER BED

The Grand Canyon has five **ecosystems**. They occur at different **elevations**. The highest elevations are along the North Rim. This area is thickly forested and has cold, snowy winters. The next-highest elevations support ponderosa pine forests along both rims. They get some snow in winter and thunderstorms in summer.

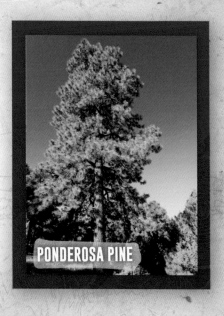

PONDEROSA PINE

GRAND CANYON'S ECOSYSTEMS

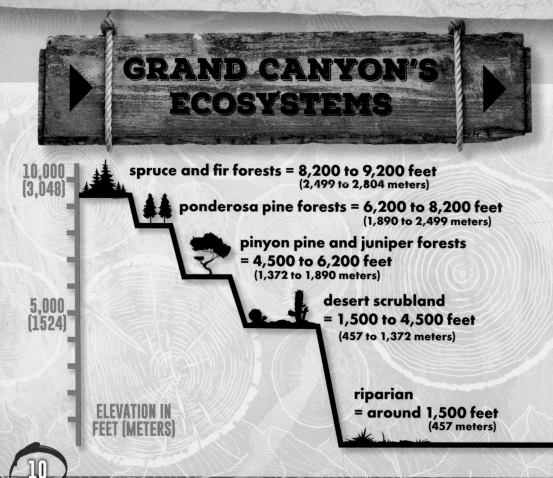

10,000
(3,048)

spruce and fir forests = 8,200 to 9,200 feet
(2,499 to 2,804 meters)

ponderosa pine forests = 6,200 to 8,200 feet
(1,890 to 2,499 meters)

pinyon pine and juniper forests
= 4,500 to 6,200 feet
(1,372 to 1,890 meters)

desert scrubland
= 1,500 to 4,500 feet
(457 to 1,372 meters)

5,000
(1524)

riparian
= around 1,500 feet
(457 meters)

ELEVATION IN
FEET (METERS)

JANUARY	APRIL
▲ HIGH: 41°F (5°C)	▲ HIGH: 60°F (16°C)
▼ LOW: 18°F (-8°C)	▼ LOW: 32°F (0°C)
JULY	OCTOBER
▲ HIGH: 84°F (29°C)	▲ HIGH: 65°F (18°C)
▼ LOW: 54°F (12°C)	▼ LOW: 39°F (4°C)

°F = degrees Fahrenheit °C = degrees Celsius

Just below the rim, short junipers and pinyon pines form another ecosystem. Here, the weather is dry with hot summers. Desert **scrubland** makes up the lowest elevations of the canyon to the canyon floor. This is the canyon's driest ecosystem. An ecosystem of lush trees and plants rises along the river. It has mild winters and very hot summers.

PLANTS AND WILDLIFE

The Grand Canyon is full of life! Each of its ecosystems is home to unique animals and plants. On the North Rim, towering spruce and fir trees mix with aspen and other trees to form thick forests. Mule deer and elk search for plants to munch, while bison wander flatter areas.

Mountain lions roam above and below the canyon rim. Kaibab squirrels chatter from ponderosa pine forests on the North Rim. Spotted owls also rest in these trees. Ringtails and bats come out at night to hunt. Condors perch on the canyon rim and search for prey below.

MULE DEER

KAIBAB SQUIRREL

MEXICAN SPOTTED OWL

MOUNTAIN LION

BISON

CALIFORNIA CONDOR

Life Span: around 60 years
Status: critically endangered

California condor range =

LEAST CONCERN	NEAR THREATENED	VULNERABLE	ENDANGERED	CRITICALLY ENDANGERED	EXTINCT IN THE WILD	EXTINCT

Inside the canyon, bighorn sheep scale the steep walls. Peregrine falcons and canyon wrens nest in the cliffs. Bobcats hide among short pinyon pines and juniper shrubs as they hunt for desert cottontails.

BIGHORN SHEEP

PEREGRINE FALCON

MOJAVE DESERT TORTOISE

Life Span: up to 80 years
Status: critically endangered

Mojave Desert
tortoise range =

LEAST CONCERN	NEAR THREATENED	VULNERABLE	ENDANGERED	CRITICALLY ENDANGERED	EXTINCT IN THE WILD	EXTINCT

In the lowest layer of the canyon, tortoises nibble on prickly pear cactuses. Collared lizards lay on rocks to bask in the sun. Pink rattlesnakes curl up between rocks. Cottonwood and willow trees shade the canyon floor. Tree frogs sing from their branches. Great blue herons wade in the waters of the Colorado River. Suckers and chubs swim below them.

HUMANS IN GRAND CANYON NATIONAL PARK

SACRED LAND

The canyon is sacred to many groups. The Zuni believe they began near the North Rim. The Hopi believe all life began in the canyon. A spring in the canyon is important to the Hopi and the Navajo.

Ancient people were living in and around the Grand Canyon more than 13,000 years ago. The Ancestral Puebloan people arrived around 2,000 years ago. They began as hunter-gatherers known for weaving beautiful baskets. Later, they began to farm and make stone homes. But they were gone by 1300 CE.

Other Native American groups soon moved into the area. The Hopi, **descendants** of the Ancestral Puebloans, were among the first. The Southern Paiute lived around the North Rim. The Havasupai and Hualapai lived in the western part of the canyon. Around 1400, the canyon became home to Navajo people.

The first Europeans arrived at the Grand Canyon in 1540. Hopi guides led García López de Cárdenas to the canyon. However, the Europeans were unable to reach the bottom. In the following centuries, few other European groups tried to explore the canyon. Then in 1869, American John Wesley Powell boated down the Colorado River and became the first white man to explore the canyon.

Following his trip, more people started coming to the area. Miners searched for gold and other valuable items. Many ended up working in **tourism** instead. Once the railroad reached the area, the canyon's popularity exploded.

MINERS

PRESIDENT
WOODROW WILSON

HOME IN THE CANYON

The Havasupai still live within the canyon walls. But they do not live within the park. Their home is in the Havasu Canyon. Many tourists visit this canyon to see its stunning waterfalls!

President Benjamin Harrison preserved the canyon as the Grand Canyon Forest Reserve in 1893. President Theodore Roosevelt later made it a national monument in 1908. Finally in 1919, President Woodrow Wilson signed the law that made it a national park. In the 1920s and 1930s, government workers created trails and other structures within the park.

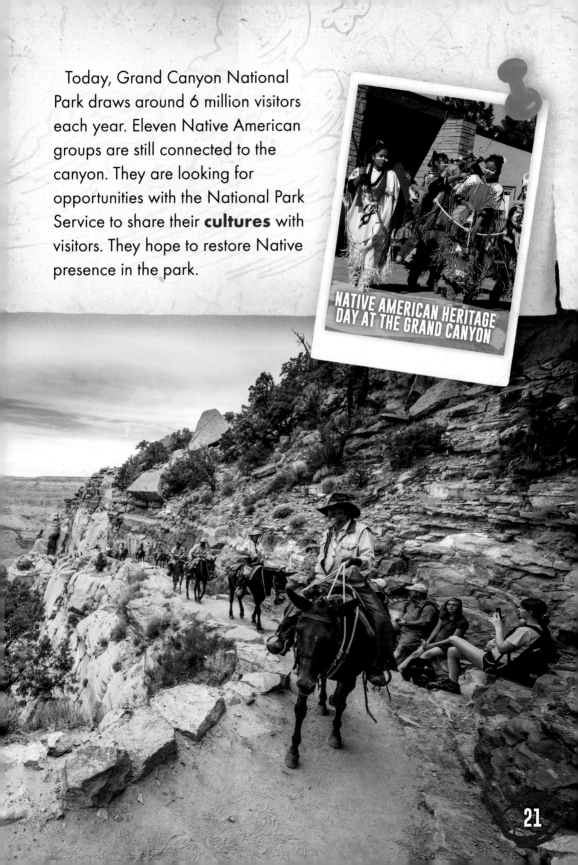

Today, Grand Canyon National Park draws around 6 million visitors each year. Eleven Native American groups are still connected to the canyon. They are looking for opportunities with the National Park Service to share their **cultures** with visitors. They hope to restore Native presence in the park.

NATIVE AMERICAN HERITAGE DAY AT THE GRAND CANYON

VISITING GRAND CANYON NATIONAL PARK

There are many ways to explore the Grand Canyon! Visitors can view the canyon by driving or biking along the rim. Many hike on the park's hundreds of miles of trails. Mule rides take visitors down to the canyon floor. Some people camp there. Rafts and **dories** take people through the canyon on the Colorado River.

CAMPING

RAFTING

TOP SITES

DESERT VIEW WATCHTOWER

PHANTOM RANCH

TUSAYAN RUIN AND MUSEUM

TUSAYAN MUSEUM

YAVAPAI GEOLOGY MUSEUM

The park offers opportunities for learning, too. Museums highlight the formation of the park and teach about Native American cultures. Ruins also reveal Native American history. Each June, visitors can appreciate the park's dark skies and learn about stars at the yearly Star Party.

PROTECTING THE PARK

The Grand Canyon faces many threats. **Uranium** mining began in nearby areas in the 1950s. Pollution from mining can run into streams that flow into the canyon. Dust in the air can harm wildlife. The Grand Canyon's popularity is also harmful. More people traveling to the area leads to more buildings and roads. This takes away natural lands. Too many hikers can erode trails and threaten wildlife.

Climate change is another major problem. Warming temperatures will make the canyon even drier. With less water available, plants and animals will be unable to survive. Frequent **droughts** also make wildfires more common. Pollution and smoke from wildfires can make it harder to see the canyon's sights.

GLEN CANYON DAM

In 1963, the Glen Canyon Dam was completed on the Colorado River near the Grand Canyon. The dam affects the Grand Canyon's ecosystems. It blocks important sediment that would be carried by the river.

Many groups are working to protect the Grand Canyon. In 2015, thousands of people wrote letters opposing a nearby development that would threaten the water supply. They stopped the development! In 2021, Arizona lawmakers worked with the Havasupai and other groups on the Grand Canyon Protection Act. This bill would ban new uranium mines.

You can help protect the park, too! Staying on the trail while visiting prevents erosion. Taking all trash with you when you leave helps keep wildlife and the environment safe. Reducing water and energy use can help limit climate change. Everyone can help keep this natural wonder safe!

DO NOT THROW ROCKS!

It can be tempting to throw a rock from the rim into the canyon. But it is dangerous and against the rules. Rocks could harm hikers or animals. They could even start a landslide!

GRAND CANYON NATIONAL PARK FACTS

 Area: **1,878** square miles (4,864 square kilometers)

 Annual Visitors: 4.5 million visitors in 2021

 Area Rank: **11**TH largest park

 Population Rank: **4**TH most visited park in 2021

 Date Designated: February 26, 1919

 Highest point: Point Imperial; 8,803 feet (2,683 meters) (North Rim)

TIMELINE

1200s
Ancestral Puebloans begin to leave the Grand Canyon area

1540
Hopi guides lead Spanish explorers to the canyon

1868
John Wesley Powell leads an expedition through the canyon by boat

FOOD WEB

BOBCAT

DESERT COTTONTAIL

ABERT'S SQUIRREL

PRICKLY PEAR CACTUS

PONDEROSA PINE

PINYON PINE

1975

The U.S. government returns 185,000 acres (749 square kilometers) of land to the Havasupai people

1919

President Woodrow Wilson signs a law establishing Grand Canyon National Park

1979

The park is made a UNESCO World Heritage Site

GREAT SEAL OF THE HAVASUPAI TRIBE 1880
HAVSUW· BAAJA

GLOSSARY

ancestral—related to relatives who lived long ago

climate change—a human-caused change in Earth's weather due to warming temperatures

cultures—beliefs, arts, and ways of life in places or societies

descendants—people related to a person or group of people who lived at an earlier time

dories—V-shaped boats with flat bottoms and high sides

droughts—long periods of dry weather

ecosystems—communities of living things that include plants, animals, and the environments around them

elevations—heights above sea level

erosion—the process through which rocks are worn away by wind, water, or ice

igneous—related to a type of rock that forms when melted rock inside the earth called magma cools

mesas—flat-topped hills

metamorphic—related to a type of rock that forms from heat and pressure

plateau—an area of flat, raised land

ravines—small, narrow valleys created by running water

reservations—areas of land that are controlled by Native American groups

runoff—rainwater and other precipitation that joins streams

scrubland—dry land that has mostly low plants and few trees

sedimentary—related to a type of rock that forms from layers of sediment that are pressed together; sediments are tiny pieces of rocks, minerals, and other natural materials.

tourism—the business of people traveling to visit other places

uranium—a radioactive element

TO LEARN MORE

AT THE LIBRARY

Grack, Rachel. *Arizona*. Minneapolis, Minn.: Bellwether Media, 2022.

Mahoney, Emily. *20 Fun Facts About the Grand Canyon*. New York, N.Y.: Gareth Stevens Publishing, 2019.

Payne, Stefanie. *National Parks: Discover All 62 Parks of the United States*. New York, N.Y.: DK Publishing, 2020.

ON THE WEB

FACTSURFER

Factsurfer.com gives you a safe, fun way to find more information.

1. Go to www.factsurfer.com.

2. Enter "Grand Canyon National Park" into the search box and click 🔍.

3. Select your book cover to see a list of related content.

INDEX